D1527139

Spring Has Come

BOOKS BY THE AUTHOR

Romance de Agapito Cascante,
Repertorio Americano, Costa Rica, 1955
The Gathering Wave,
Alan Swallow, Denver, 1961
The Flesh of Utopia,
Alan Swallow, Denver, 1964
Menashtash,
Little Square Book Review, Santa Barbara, 1969
Agapito,
Charles Scribners' Sons, New York, 1969
Spain, Let This Cup Pass From Me, (Cesar Vallejo),
translations, Red Hill Press, 1972
Words on Paper,
Red Hill Press, Los Angeles, 1974
Two Elegies,
Red Hill Press, Los Angeles, 1976
The Half-Eaten Angel,
Nodin Press, Minneapolis, 1981
When I Was a Father,
New Rivers Press, Saint Paul, 1982
Miss O'Keeffe (Collaboration),
University of New Mexico Press, Albuquerque, 1992
Four Poems About Sparrows,
Eyelight Press, Cordoba, 1994
A Garden of Sound,
Pemmican Press, Washington, 1996
A History of Light,
Sherman Asher Publishing, Santa Fe, 1997
Thirteen Tangos for Stravinsky,
Sherman Asher Publishing, Santa Fe, 1999

Spring Has Come

SPANISH LYRICAL POETRY FROM THE SONGBOOKS OF THE RENAISSANCE

Alvaro Cardona-Hine

La Alameda Press :: Albuquerque

ISBN: 1-888809-20-5
Library of Congress Control #: 00-134030

La Alameda Press
9636 Guadalupe Trail NW
Albuquerque, New Mexico 87114

La primavera ha venido,
nadie sabe como ha sido.

Antonio Machado

Spring has come,
nobody knows how it's happened.

The Discovery of Spanish Lyrical Poetry and Other Matters

One could not have found a better title for this collection of old Spanish poems than Machado's "Spring has come" if only because, as with the season itself and until very recently, nobody knew how Spanish lyrical poetry had come into being. Well could the philologist at the turn of the century have exclaimed, "nobody knows how it's happened!"

For a long time, criticism has assumed that Spanish poetry was preponderably epic. Those little flowers in the Songbooks of the Renaissance, shadowed in the crannies of such mountains as the *Cantar del Mio Cid* had, seemingly, no roots that anyone could discover. They were a puzzle to those great men of Spanish letters, Menendez Pelayo and Menendez Pidal who, at the beginning of this century, gave their attention to the problem.

Menendez Pelayo was the first to realize, with a sudden shock of delighted awareness, that a popular lyric poetry had somehow existed all along, its origins sunk deep in the Middle Ages. But he had no way to prove any of this, and he could only insist on the importance and beauty of this poetry.

It took nerve for a great philologist like Ramón Menéndez Pidal to theorize that the perfect little lyrics that appear in the 15th and 16th centuries in Castilian, and which are later utilized by such superb poets as Gil Vicente and Lope de Vega, obeyed a long tradition, when only the barest hints existed.

His thesis, based on old chronicles and on those later-day lyrics, was verified when Arabian scholars began to point to the Andalusian-Moorish basis for some of the forms and themes in the work of the Galicians, Portuguese, Italians and Spaniards. But while in 1919 Menéndez Pidal could only surmise that Castilian and Galician-Portuguese lyrics could have a common root (such as the *zejel* with its two line, rhymed refrain, and its four line stanza with a same rhyme for the first three and the rhyme of the refrain for the fourth), the discovery of some *jarchas* came to prove him right and to underwrite just how ancient the Spanish lyrical vein really was.

It all happened in a rather novel way when the Semitist S.M. Stern published a collection of 20 *muguasajas* (sometimes spelled *moaxajas* or *muwassahas*) with Mozarabic *jarchas*. The *muguasaja* is a poem with a structure somewhat like that of the *zejel* but written in classical Arabian. One of its characteristics is that it must end with a couplet in the vernacular, or jargon, or in a romance language. This couplet is what is called the *jarcha*. The *jarcha* was all important; its choice determined everything else in the *muguasaja*.

It has been claimed that the *muguasaja* was the invention of the blind 9th century poet Muccáddam ben Muáfa but in actuality it is an Andalusian romanic form which he simply incorporated into Arabic poetry. The presentation by Stern of *muguasajas* written by Spanish Jews using Mozarabic *jarchas* revolutionized research. As Jose María Alín, a student of traditional Spanish poetry puts it, "…the discovery is sensational. These refrains, whose date is not always certain and whose interpretation is extremely difficult, go much further back than Provençal poetry, considered the oldest lyrical poetry in a Romance language." (See *El Cancionero Español de Tipo Tradicional*, Jose María Alín, Taurus, Madrid, 1968).

Since the *jarcha* had to be a popular couplet in street language, not many poets could, or bothered to, invent their own. They simply borrowed them from other poets or, as Stern himself states, "It seems that in their origin, the verses of the *jarcha* must have been taken from popular romanic poetry." (Quoted in Alín's book already cited). We must add that they were likewise foreign to Hebrew and Arabic poetry in that they used assonant rhyme.

Ibn Sana al Mulk, who died in the early part of the 13th century, says, "Some poets, being incapable of composing a good *jarcha*, take another's, which is better than if they had attempted to write one themselves and have it prove weak."

The oldest *jarcha* to date is that of a certain Joseph el Escriba, who celebrates events of the year 1042 in a *muguasaja*. This, let us note in passing, is one hundred years before the estimated date of the Poema del Cid and earlier than the work of the first Provençal troubadour, William IX of Aquitaine.

A reading of that delightful book, *The Structure of Spanish History*, by Americo Castro, is enough to convince anyone of the intense conviviality of the Christian, the Moorish and Jewish cultures in the Spain before Isabella and Ferdinand. It prepares one to understand how Jewish poets could have taken to the native forms. Furthermore, the Jews were apparently more concerned with or more fortunate in the preservation of their poetry than Christian or Moor, and it is thanks to this fact that we have the *jarchas* borrowed from the living fountain of a people's oral tradition.

After such a discovery it was possible for students to quit worrying about the relationship between the *zejel* and Spanish poetry. As Dámaso Alonso, poet and scholar, puts it, "Let us say it once and for all: The center of interest must be shifted from the *zejel* to the *villancico*. (*Jarcha* equals *villancico*) These examples of Mozarabic *villancicos* from the 11th century, placed alongside the entire Castilian tradition of a later day, prove perfectly that the popular lyric nucleus of the hispanic tradition is a brief and simple stanza: a *villancico*." (See *Antología de la Poesía Española, Poesía de Tipo Tradicional*, Dámaso Alonso y Jose M. Blecua, Antología Hispánica, Madrid, 1956)

The majority of the poems translated here appeared in *cancioneros* between 1511 and 1605. Prior to that time, poets and scriveners disdained what the common people were singing.

And how long had the people been singing?

"Estrabon mentions the choral chants of the Lusitanians, accompanied by flutes and trumpets," says Jose María Alín (opus cited). "Silvio Itálico refers to the dances of the Galicians, very similar, by what he says, to the *danza prima*; Valerio Marcial speaks of the Andalusian female minstrels, and the *puella gaditana* mentioned by Juvenal is quite well known."

Menéndez Pidal, quoted by Alín, speaks of " ... The councils and the ecclessiastical writers from the 6th century on, telling us of the clumsy and indecorous love songs heard among the people; they only note the immorality of such songs, but it must be obvious that there also existed impeccable, noble songs, if only because these had no reason to be mentioned by the clergy, who were solely preoccupied with correcting harmful notions."

When the traditional poetry began to appear in the *cancioneros*, of course, it meant that the poets and musicians had begun to take an interest in it and to use it as the basis for their own inspiration. As Alín says, "What is initiated with the *Cancionero Musical de Palacio* and Juan de Encina, is molded into a marvelous reality with the Portuguese poet (Gil Vicente, who also wrote in Spanish) and will reach its greatest splendor with the Madrid dramaturgist (Lope de Vega)."

However, not much attention, other than literary, has been given the actual content of these songs. There is a truly remarkable fact hidden—and hidden only because we have been overwhelmingly chauvinistic in our approach. In a goodly number of these traditional poems the voice heard is the voice of the female, of woman in her womanly condition. And yet, to our knowledge, no one has gone from there to recognize that perhaps, quite simply and logically, the creators *were* women.

Menéndez Pidal characterizes primitive Andalusian songs, the *cantigas de amigo* and the Castilian *villancicos* as three branches of one poetic fervor: "The three varieties have the air of belonging to one unmistakable family and, above all, the three of them possess at their best a double affinity in being songs placed in the mouth of a girl in love and having that girl confidentially close to her mother." (Alín, op. cit.)

Note the words 'placed in the mouth of a girl.' Implied is the notion that, naturally, the songs were invented by men and 'placed' in the mouths of girls. Just as if, centuries from now, and with practically no records available, scholars were to speak of the *blues* as being 'placed' in the mouths of blacks because the notion that the blacks could have been the actual creators and singers would not have occurred to them.

Coming from the grand old man of Spanish philology, those words merely indicate how deeply conditioned we are in accepting roles foisted upon us by society. Couldn't it be that, given the extraordinary quality of life in Spain during the second millenium A.D., women of the peasantry sang of their affairs just as the men sang of theirs, and just as they worked the fields alongside the male?

It seems impossible that men could have created all of these lovely lyrics. There is such a palpitating awareness of what it means to be a woman in some of them that it should give us pause. And when we go to the poems actually written by known poets (a few will be found at the end of this volume) we see a difference. Some assume the position and stance of the woman, obviously out of sympathy and because the theme was dramatically attractive, but they never have the immediacy of the anonymous poems.

It would be enormously interesting if scholars were to investigate this matter in depth. The scope of the present volume precludes more than mention of the problem. However, one of the reasons in offering these poems to the public is connected with this whole issue of male and female reality-roles underlying present-day consciousness. We are quick in our century to sense and see everything in political terms, to abstract the most personal issues and turn them into slogans, even in poetry. We seldom see how this divides us further. These poems from old Spain are poems, not of political protest, but of the protest of the senses, and therefore of a real facing of the issue: man-woman harmony.

Just as our poetry is often colorless or merely strident and suicidal, so our lives tend to be drab and listless. I recall reading a group of these translations at a literary gathering and getting little reaction. I saw that the sexual allusions of some of the simplest poems were going over the heads of the audience, sophisticated twentieth century people. To them, a two-line poem such as:

> Under the hill blooms the rose
> that the air does not scorch.

was apparently only a poem about a hill and a rose. Finally, I said something about the subtle erotic flavor of the songs. It was as if my listeners had to be awakened. From that point on, I hardly have to say it, everyone perked up and began to listen more carefully. And so, perhaps, these songs will tell us that there are lovely ways to deal with experience.

I have placed the songs which I felt were most clearly created and sung by women in the first grouping. These are followed by those of a more indeterminate nature and then those more apparently created by men. The reader might quarrel with specific choices but I hope that, in the main, he or she will agree with me. At the end I have placed the famed and lovely "Plaint on the Death of Guillen Peraza," two Judeo-Spanish songs (one female, one male) and some poems in the traditional style but written by known poets of the Renaissance.

The Spanish text has been left as found in the original sources. The spelling is sometimes startlingly novel and contradictory, even within the same poem, but since nothing is clearly unintelligible, original spellings have been respected throughout.

In translating I have followed the line of least resistance, rhyming where possible and, in general, trying to preserve the spirit and verve of each poem. In a few instances I have attempted to hew to a rhyming scheme in a longer lyric. This is usually a dangerous procedure because the result, in terms of actual imagery, is seldom close to the original. I simply wanted, in these cases, to convey the feeling of the old forms.

Alvaro Cardona-Hine
Truchas, New Mexico

for Mario Espinoza
and the others

Part I

Besóme el colmenero,
que a la miel me supo el beso.

The beekeeper kissed me,
the kiss it tasted like honey.

Al alba venid, buen amigo,
al alba venid.

Amigo el que yo más quería,
venid al alba del dia.

Amigo el que yo más amaba,
venid a la luz del alba.

Venid a la luz del día,
non trayáis compañía.

Venid a la luz del alba,
non traigáis gran compaña.

Come at dawn, good friend,
come at dawn.

Friend I wanted most,
come at break of day.

Friend I loved best,
come at crack of dawn.

Come at crack of day,
bring no one.

Come at crack of dawn,
bring no one at all.

Que no me desnudéys,
amores de mi vida;
que no me desnudéys,
que yo me yré en camisa.

Entrastes, mi señora,
en el huerto ageno,
cogistes tres pericas
del peral del medio,
dexárades la prenda
d'amor verdadero.
Que no me desnudéys,
que yo me yré en camisa.

Don't undress me,
love of my life;
don't undress me,
let me go in my slip.

You came, my lady,
into the stranger's orchard,
took three little pears
from the center tree;
now you must leave us
proof of your love.
Don't undress me,
let me go in my slip.

Feridas tenéis, amigo,
y duélenos;
tuviéralas yo, y no vos.

You come wounded, love,
and it pains us;
would that it were me and not you.

En Avila, mis ojos,
dentro de Avila.

En Avila del Río
mataron a mi amigo,
dentro de Avila.

In Avila, I saw it,
inside Avila.

In Avila del Rio
they murdered my love,
inside Avila.

Llueve menudico
y hace la noche escura,
el pastorcillo es nuevo,
non iré segura.

It drizzles,
the night is dark;
he's a new shepherd,
I don't feel at ease.

Aquel pastorcico, madre,
que no viene,
algo tiene en el campo
que le duele.

That shepherd, Mother,
who hasn't shown up,
something must pain him
out in the fields.

Al coger amapolas,
madre, me perdí;
¡caras amapolas
fueron para mí!

Picking poppies,
Mother, I was lost;
oh, the price I had to pay
for those poppies!

De iglesia en iglesia
me quiero yo andar
por no malmaridar.

From church to church
I'd rather hop
than wed him and flop.

¿Agora que sé d'amor me metéis monja?
¡Ay, Dios, qué grave cosa!

Agora que sé d'amor de caballero,
agora me metéis monja en el monesterio.
¡Ay, Dios, qué grave cosa!

Now I've tasted love you'd make me a nun?
Oh, God, what an awful blunder!

Now that I know the love of man,
now you shut me in a cell.
Oh, God, what an awful blunder!

Mongica en religión me quiero entrar
por no malmaridar.

I'd rather see myself a nun in church
than a wife left in the lurch.

A mi puerta nace una fonte,
¿por dó saliré que no me moje?

A mi puerta la garrida
nasce una fonte frida
donde lavo la mi camisa
y la de aquel que yo más quería.
¿Por dó saliré que no me moje?

At my doorstep springs a fountain.
How to get out and not get wet?

At my handsome doorstep
springs a cold fountain
where I wash my shirt
and that of the one I loved best.
How to get out and not get wet?

De tu cama a la mía
pasa un varquillo;
aventúrate y pasa,
moreno mío.

There's a boat sailing
from your bed to mine;
take a chance and come over,
my sunburnt lover.

Yo, madre, yo,
que la flor de la villa me só.

Me, Mother, me;
the pick of the village is no one but me.

Mírame, Miguel,
cómo estoy bonica:
saya de buriel,
camisa de estopica.

Michael, look at me,
how pretty I look
in my kersey skirt,
in my cambric blouse.

No sé qué me bulle
en el calcañar,
que no puedo andar.

Yéndome y viniendo
a las mis vacas,
no sé qué me bulle
entre las faldas,
que no puedo andar.
No sé qué me bulle
en el calcañar.

God knows, it's some itch I have
in the ball of my foot;
I can hardly walk.

Coming and going
to where my cows graze,
God knows, it's some itch I have
under my skirts;
I can hardly walk.
God knows, it's some itch I have
in the ball of my foot.

Exe, Perro, no me encandiles,
que yo encandiladita me estoy.

Shoo, dog, don't bedazzle me,
I'm lightheaded enough already.

A Salamanca, el escolarillo,
a Salamanca irás.

Irás a do no te vean,
ni te escuchen ni te crean,
pues a las que te desean
tan ingrato pago das.
A Salamanca, el escolarillo,
A salamanca irás.

To Salamanca, you crazy student,
to Salamanca you'll go.

You'll go where you won't be seen,
heard or believed,
since with such hard coin
you repay those who would have you.
To Salamanca, you crazy student,
to Salamanca you'll go.

— Si jugastes anoche, amore.
— Non, señora, none.

— Did you chance to play last night, my love?
— No, my lady, no.

— Dime, pajarito que estás en el nido:
¿La dama besada pierde marido?
— No, la mi señora, si fué en escondido.

— Tell me, little bird in your nest:
Does a kiss risk a lady's husband?
— No, my lady, not if it's done under cover.

Soñaba yo que tenía
alegre mi corazón,
mas a la fe, madre mía,
que los sueños, sueños son.

I dreamt
that my heart was happy,
but by my faith, Mother,
dreams are just dreams.

Mis ojuelos, madre,
valen una ciudade.

Mis ojuelos, madre,
tanto son de claros,
cada vez que los alzo
merescen ducados,
ducados, mi madre:
valen una ciudade.

Mis ojuelos, madre,
tanto son de veros,
cada vez que los alzo
merescen dineros,
dineros, mi madre:
valen una ciudade.

My two little eyes, Mother,
they are worth a whole city.

My two little eyes, Mother,
there's so much light in them
that each time I lift them
pieces of eight they should get me,
pieces of eight, my mother,
they are worth a whole city.

My two little eyes, Mother,
have so much of you in them
that each time I lift them
monies they should get me,
monies, my mother,
they are worth a whole city.

Niña y viña, peral y habar,
malo es de guardar.

Levantéme, oh madre,
mañanica frida,
fuí a cortar la rosa,
(la rosa) florida.
Malo es de guardar.

Levantéme, oh madre,
mañanica clara,
fuí cortar la rosa,
la rosa granada.
Malo es de guardar.

Viñadero malo
prenda me pedía;
dile yo un cordone,
dile yo mi cinta.
Malo es de guardar.

Viñadero malo
prenda me demanda,
dile yo un (cordone,
dile yo una banda.
Malo es de guardar.)

Girl and vineyard,
pear orchard and bean row,
these are hard to keep.

I got up, Mother,
with the cold dawn,
went to cut a rose,
the flowering rose.
These are hard to keep.

I got up, Mother,
with the clear dawn,
went to cut a rose,
the crimson rose.
These are hard to keep.

That nasty vinekeeper
was after a pledge,
I gave him a belt,
I gave him a ribbon.
These are hard to keep.

That nasty vinekeeper
is after a pledge,
I gave him a belt,
I gave him a band.
These are hard to keep.

Van y vienen las olas, madre,
a las orillas del mar:
mi pena con las que vienen,
mi bien con las que van.

The waves come and go, Mother,
at the edge of the sea:
sorrows with those that come,
pleasures with those that go.

Part II

Pasas por mi calle,
no me quieres ver:
corazón de acero
debes de tener.

You pass down my street
but won't look my way;
you must have
a heart of steel.

No puedo apartarme
de los amores, madre,
no puedo apartarme.

Amor tiene aquesto
con su lindo gesto,
que prende muy presto
y suelta muy tarde:
no puedo apartarme.

I can't forfeit
love, Mother,
I can't let it go.

When it seems to have
the lightest touch
is when it grabs
and won't let go:
I can't forfeit love.

Si lo dicen, digan,
alma mía,
si lo dicen, digan.

Dicen que vos quiero
y por vos me muero;
dicho es verdadero,
alma mía,
si lo dicen, digan.

If they say it, let them,
dear soul,
if they say it, let them.

They say I love you
to death;
true enough,
dear soul,
if they say it, let them.

Mano a mano los dos amores,
mano a mano.

El galán y la galana
ambos vuelven el agua clara,
mano a mano.

Hand in hand the two lovers,
hand in hand.

The young man and his girl,
they turn the water to light,
hand in hand.

Aquel pajecito de aquel plumaje,
aguilica sería quien lo alcanzase.

Aquel pajecito de los airones,
que volando lleva los corazones,
aguilica sería quien le alcanzase.

That bird of wild plumage,
it'd take a hawk to catch it.

That bird tumbling in air,
taking my heart to its lair,
it'd take a hawk to catch it.

Lleva un pastorcico
cubierto el cuidado
de muy enamorado.

That shepherd
goes around hiding
the fact that he's smitten.

Campanillas de Toledo,
óigoos y no vos veo.

Little bells of Toledo,
I hear you and cannot see you.

Veo que todos se quejan,
yo callando moriré.

Everybody complains;
I will die silent.

¿Cuándo, mas cuándo
llevará cerecicas el cardo?

When, but when
will cherries grow on the thistle?

Las ondas del mar,
¡cuán menudicas van!

The waves of the sea,
see how close they go!

Ojos que no ven
lo que ver desean,
¿qué verán que vean?

Eyes that don't see
what they really want to,
what would they see if they saw?

Dejadme llorar,
orillas de la mar.

Let me weep
at the edge of the deep.

Este es el camino del cielo,
este es el camino de allá.

This is the road to heaven,
this is their road.

Gavilán que andáis de noche,
¿qué viento corre?

Hawk, you that fly with the night,
is it windy?

Turbias van las aguas, madre,
turbias van;
mas ellas se aclararán.

The waters run muddy, Mother,
muddy they run;
but they will clear up.

La niña gritillos dar
no es de maravillar.

Mucho grita la cuitada
con la voz desmesurada
por se veer asalteada;
non es de maravillar.

Amor puro la venció
que a muchas engañó,
si por el se descibió
no es de maravillar.

Temprano quiso saber
el trabajo e placer
qu'el amor non faz haber;
non es de maravillar.

A los diez años complidos
fueron d'ella conocidos
todos sus cinco sentidos;
non es de maravillar.

A los quince ¿qué fará?
Esto notar se debrá
por quien la practicará;
non es de maravillar.

The girl lets out a scream,
not so strange as it might seem.

She's yelling, making noise
in a high-pitched voice
that she's had no choice;
not so strange as it might seem.

True love has had its way,
it's fooled many in its day;
she's picked him, so they say;
not so strange as it might seem.

She came early to know
how it's pleasure and woe
are the knots in love's bow;
not so strange as it might seem.

At ten she's painted,
already acquainted,
her five senses tainted;
not so strange as it might seem.

At fifteen, what will she do?
Think it over who might sue,
is it something you might rue?
Not so strange as it might seem.

Part III

Yéndome y viniendo
me fuí namorando,
una vez riendo
y otra vez llorando.

Yo estaba sin veros
de amor descuydado,
mas en conoceros
me vi namorado.
Nunca mi cuidado
se va moderando,
una vez riendo
y otra vez llorando.

Sentí gran tormento
de verme perdido,
mas estoy contento,
pues por vos ha sido;
el mal es crecido
y ha d'irse pasando,
una vez riendo
y otra vez llorando.

Otro mayor mal
me tiene ya muerto,
es tal que por cierto
no tiene su ygual;
tiéneme ya tal
que me va acabando,
una vez riendo
y otra vez llorando.

How I fell in love
was coming and going,
sometimes laughing,
sometimes crying.

Before I saw you
I could have cared less,
once it happened
I couldn't care more.
I never seem to hew
to the middle road,
sometimes laughing,
sometimes crying.

I couldn't believe
I was in such trouble
because I was happy
that you were the cause;
if the mischief grows
it will come to pass,
sometimes laughing,
sometimes crying.

A new trouble has me
right over the barrel,
the size of the mess
you'll find nowhere else;
if it gets much worse
it might do me in,
sometimes laughing,
sometimes crying.

En Cañatañazor
perdió Almançor
ell atamor.

In Cañatañazor
love went out the door
for Almançor.

Páreste a la ventana,
niña en cabello,
que otro parayso
yo no lo tengo.

Stand by the window, girl,
naked, if you will;
that another such heaven
I shall never have.

Ya os tengo, peces,
en las redes.

Now I've caught you, fishes,
in my net.

Baxo de la peña nace
la rosa que no quema el ayre.

Under the hill blooms the rose
that the air does not scorch.

En aquella peña, en aquella,
que no caben en ella.

In that hillock, that one,
there's no room for so many.

Este pradico verde,
trillémosle y hollémosle.

This little green meadow,
let's cut us a path
and do some planting.

Lindos ojos la garza,
y no los alza.

The heron, what eyes!
but she won't lift them.

¡A la gala de la panadera,
a la gala della,
a la gala della
y del pan que lleva!

Here's to the baker girl
with the fancy airs,
with the fancy airs
peddling bread with a flair!

Desciende al valle, la niña.
Non era de día.

Niña de rubios cabellos,
desciende a los corderos
que andan por los centenos.
Non era de día.

She's down to the valley, the girl.
And not yet day.

Blond girl
down among the sheep
feeding in the rye.
And not yet day.

Oxalá fuese, señora mía,
oxalá fuese lo que no es.

I wish, my lady,
I wish for what isn't.

Isabel, Isabel,
perdiste la tu faja;
hela por do va
nadando por el agua.
¡Isabel, la tan garrida!

Isabel, Isabel,
you've lost your belt;
see, there it goes
floating on the water.
Isabel, pretty girl!

Este coraçón mío
abierto por el medio
dalde, señora, remedio.

This heart
you've split open,
find balm for it, lady.

Caracoles avéys comido
y mal os han hecho;
menester os avéys de sangrar
de la vena del pecho.

You've eaten snails
and they haven't settled;
maybe we'll have to bleed
a vein in your chest.

Que miraba la mar
la mal casada,
que miraba la mar
cómo es ancha y larga.

She kept watching the sea,
the mismatched wife;
she kept watching the sea,
how long it is and wide.

Por el mar de mis ojos
pasando a nado,
encontré la sirena
de mis cuidados.

Swimming across
the sea of my eyes
I found the siren
of all my sighs.

Perricos de mi señora,
no me mordades agora.

Pups of my lady,
do not bite me now.

Yo me yva, mi madre,
a Villa Reale,
errara yo el camino
en fuerte lugare.

Siete días anduve
que no comí pane,
cevada mi mula,
carne el gavilán.
Entre la Zarçuela
y Daracután,
alçara los ojos
hazia do el sol sale;
viera una cabaña,
della el humo sale.
Picara mi mula,
fuyme para allá;
perros del ganado
salenme a ladrar;
vide una serrana
del bello donaire.

— Llegaos, cavallero,
verguença no ayades;
mi padre y mi madre
ha ydo al lugar,
mi caro Minguillo
es ydo por pan,
ni vendrá esta noche
ni mañana a yantar;
comereys de la leche
mientras el queso se haze.
Haremos la cama

I was on my way, Mother,
to Villa Reale,
when I took the wrong turn
through a desolate place.

For seven days
I tasted no bread,
the mule no barley,
the hawk no meat.
Between Zarçuela
and Daracután
I happened to glance
at the rising sun
when I saw a hut
and a wisp of smoke.
Spurring the mule
to get there fast
I was surrounded
by barking dogs
till a girl showed up
pretty as could be.

Welcome, Sir,
let's not feel ashamed;
my father and mother
are presently away,
and my own Minguillo
has gone to get bread;
he won't be returning
tonight or tomorrow;
you shall have some milk
while the cheese gets ripe.
We shall make our bed

junto al retamal;
haremos un hijo,
llamarse ha Pasqual;
o será Arçobispo,
Papa o Cardenal,
o será porquerizo
de Villa Real.
Bien, por vida mía,
deveys de burlar!

where the furze grows wild,
beget us a son
we shall call Pascual
to be either archbishop,
cardinal or pope,
or merely a swineherd
of the Villa Real.
Sweet, on my life,
take advantage!

Rodrigo Martínez
a las ánsares, ¡ahe!,
pensando qu'eran vacas
silbábalas: ¡He!

Rodrigo Martínez,
atán garrido,
los tus ansarinos
liévalos al río, ¡ahe!
Pensando qu'eran vacas
silbábalas: ¡He!

Rodrigo Martínez,
atán lozano,
los tus ansarinos
liévalos al vado, ¡ahe!
Pensando qu'eran vacas
silbábalas: ¡He!

Rodrigo Martínez,
to your geese, Hey there!
He whistles at them
as if they were cows, hey!

Rodrigo Martínez,
you handsome fellow,
see that you drive
your goslings to water, Hey there!
He whistles at them
as if they were cows, Hey!

Rodrigo Martínez,
you healthy fellow,
see that you drive
your goslings to shallows, Hey there!
He whistles at them
as if they were cows, Hey!

Dícenme que tengo amiga
y no lo sé;
por sabello moriré.

Dícenme que tengo amiga
de dentro de aquesta villa,
y aunque está en esta bailía
y no lo sé,
por sabello moriré.

Dícenme que tengo amada
de dentro de aquesta plaza,
y que está en esta baila
y no lo sé,
por sabello moriré.

They tell me that I have a friend
and I don't know it; God,
I am dying to know it.

They tell me a girl likes me
living in this town
and though she's in this neighborhood
I don't know it; Lord,
I am dying to know it.

They tell me that I have a lover
this side of the main square,
that she's here at this dance
and I don't know it; God,
I am dying to know it.

Part IV

Llorad las damas, si Dios os vala,
Guillén Peraza quedó en la Palma,
la flor marchita de la su cara.

No eres palma, eres retama,
eres ciprés de triste rama,
eres desdicha, desdicha mala.

Tus campos rompan tristes volcanes,
no vean placeres, sino pesares,
cubran tus flores los arenales.

Guillén Peraza, Guillén Peraza,
¿dó está tu escudo, dó está tu lanza?
Todo lo acaba la malandanza.

Weep, ladies, for God's grace,
Guillén Peraza won't leave this place,
flowers of Palma wilt on his face.

Instead of a standard you're the lowly broom,
branch of cypress buried in gloom,
misfortune, nothing but doom.

May brimstone lay waste to your land,
no pleasure fall to the hand,
but flowers drowning in sand.

Guillén Peraza, Guillén Peraza,
where is your shield, where is your lance?
Everything ends in mischance.

Fuérame a bañar
a orías del río,
aí encontrí, madre,
a mi lindo amigo:
él me dió un abrazo,
yo le di sinco.

Fuérame a bañar
a oría de claro,
aí encontrí, madre,
a mi lindo amado:
él me dió un abrazo,
yo le di cuatro.

I went to bathe
at the river bank,
and there I found, Mother,
my darling friend:
he gave me a hug,
I gave him five.

I went to bathe
at the clearing's edge,
and there I found, Mother,
my darling love:
he gave me a hug,
I gave him four.

Judeo-Spanish Song

Debajo del limón
dormía la niña,
y sus pies en el agua fría.
Su amor por aí vendría:
— ¿Qué hases, mi novia garrida?
— Asperando a vos, mi vida,
lavando vuestra camisa
con xabón y lexía.
Debajo del limón, la niña,
sue pies en el agua fría:
su amor por aí vendría.

Beneath the lemon tree
slept the girl,
her feet in the cold water
till her love came by:
— What are you up to, my darling bride?
— Waiting for you, my life,
washing your shirt
with soap and lye.
The girl beneath the lemon tree,
her feet in the cold wwater
till her love came by.

Judeo-Spanish Song

Quiero ir morar al monte
solo, sin más compañía
que la tierra y su agua fría.

I want to go live in the hills
alone, with no other company
than the earth and its cold water.

Alvarez Pereira

No me las enseñes más,
que me matarás.

Estábase la monja
en el monesterio,
sus teticas blancas
de so el velo negro,
¡Más,
que me matarás!

Don't let me see them again,
for you'll kill me.

Nun
in your nunnery,
little white tits
under black veils:
Again,
for you'll kill me!

Diego Sanchez de Badajoz

Pues todas las aves vuelan, corazón,
pues todas las aves vuelan,
volad vos.

All the birds fly, heart,
all the birds fly,
so you try.

Juan de Timoneda

Dime, señora, di,
si te acordarás de mí.

Tell me, lady, tell me,
if you still remember me.

Juan Alvarez Gato

Solíades venir, amor;
agora non venides, non.

You used to come by, love;
now you never do, no.

Juan Alvarez Gato

Mal herido me ha la niña,
no me hacen justicia.

The girl has wounded me badly,
is there any justice?

Gil Vicente

Arrimárame a ti, rosa,
no me diste solombra…

I drew near you, rosebush,
nor is shade all you gave me.

Gil Vicente

CANTIGA

¡Muy graciosa es la doncella,
cómo es bella y hermosa!

Digas tu, el marinero
que en las naves vivías,
si la nave o la vela o la estrella
es tan bella.

Digas tu, el caballero
que las armas vestías,
si el caballo o las armas o la guerra
es tan bella.

Digas tu, el pastorcico
que el ganadico guardas,
si el ganado o los valles o la sierra
es tan bella.

Gil Vicente

CANTIGA

How adorable a girl,
how lovely, how beautiful!

Tell me, sailor,
you who've sailed in ships,
if ship or sail or star
is as lovely.

Tell me, knight,
you who bore arms,
if horse or arms or war
is as lovely.

Tell me, shepherd,
you who watch over flocks,
if flock or valley or mountain
is as lovely.

Gil Vicente

¿Cuál es la niña
que coge las flores
si no tiene amores?

Cogía la niña
la rosa florida,
el hortelanico
prendas le pedía,
si no tiene amores.

Show me the girl
who goes picking flowers
when she's not in love.

The girl was picking
the flowering rose,
the gardener begging
for a little sign,
when she's not in love.

Gil Vicente

COLOPHON

Set in *Bulmer*, a typeface revived for
American Type Founders in 1928 by Morris Benton
& based on the designs of William Martin,
who learned type cutting under John Baskerville
in the late 18th century. Martin later came to work
for William Bulmer's Shakespeare Press in London
for whom he contributed almost exclusively.
Utilitarian but handsome, it's sharp contrasts
have a peculiar elegance rightly suited for poetry.

Book design by J. Bryan

Alvaro Cardona-Hine, writer, painter, and composer, was born in Costa Rica in 1926 and came to the United States when he was thirteen years old. His work has been published in fourteen books of poetry, prose, and translation, and over sixty literary and national journals and numerous anthologies. He has been the recipient of a NEA grant, a Bush Foundation Fellowship, and a Minnesota Arts Board grant. He began his serious study of Zen Buddhism in 1967, which informs all his creative work: writing, musical composition, and painting. He makes his living as a painter, selling his work from his gallery/home in Truchas, New Mexico.